A Letter from Origen to Africanus

A Letter from Origen to Africanus

Written by Origen (A.D 185-254)
Translated by: Rev. Frederick Crombie D.D. (1872)
Updated to Modern US English by: Andrew Overett (2016)

A Letter from Origen to Africanus

© Lighthouse Publishing 2018

Written by Origen (A.D 185-254)
Translated by: Rev. Frederick Crombie D.D. (1872)
Updated to Modern US English by: Andrew Overett (2016)

All rights reserved. Without limiting the rights under copyright reserved above, no part of this publication may be reproduced, stored in a retrieval system, or transmitted, in any form or by any means (electronic, mechanical, photocopying, recording or otherwise), without the prior written permission of the copyright owner of this book.

Published by
Lighthouse Christian Publishing
SAN 257-4330
5531 Dufferin Drive
Savage, Minnesota, 55378
United States of America

www.lighthousechristianpublishing.com

Introductory Note to the Works of Origen.

[a.d. 185–230–254.] The reader will remember the rise and rapid development of the great Alexandrian school, and the predominance which was imparted to it by the genius of the illustrious Clement. But in Origen, his pupil, who succeeded him at the surprising age of eighteen, a new sun was to rise upon its noontide. Truly was Alexandria "the mother and mistress of churches" in the benign sense of a nurse and instructress of Christendom, not its arrogant and usurping imperatrix.

The full details of Origen's troubled but glorious career are given by Dr. Crombie, who in my opinion deserves thanks for the kind and apologetic temper of his estimate of the man and the sublime doctor, as well as of the period of his life. Upon the fervid spirit of a confessor in an age of cruelty, lust, and heathenism, what right have we to sit in judgment? Of one whose very errors were virtues at their source, how can a Christian of our self-indulgent times presume to speak in censure? Well might the Psalmist exclaim, "Let us fall now into the hand of the Lord; for His mercies are great: let me not fall into the hand of man."

A Letter from Origen to Africanus

Justly has it been urged that to those whose colossal labors during the Ante-Nicene period exposed them to hasty judgment, and led them into mistakes, much indulgence must be shown. The language of theology was but assuming shape under their processes, and we owe them an incalculable debt of gratitude: but it was not yet molded into precision; nor had great councils, presided over by the Holy Ghost, as yet afforded those safeguards to freedom of thought which gradually defined the limits of orthodoxy. To no single teacher did the Church defer. Holy Scripture and the *quod ab omnibus* were the grand *prescription*, against which no individual prelate or doctor could prevail, against which no see could uplift a voice, without chastisement and subjection. Over and over again were the bishops of patriarchal and apostolic sees, including Rome, adjudged heretics, and anathematized by the inexorable law of truth, and of "the faith once delivered to the saints," which not even "an angel from heaven" might presume to change or to enlarge. But before the great Synodical period (a.d. 325 to 451), while orthodoxy is marvelously maintained and witnessed to by Origen and Tertullian themselves, their errors, however serious, have never separated them from the grateful and loving regard of those upon whom their lives of heroic sorrow and suffering have conferred blessings unspeakable. The Church cannot leave their errors uncorrected. Their persons she leaves to the Master's award: their characters she cherishes, while their faults she deplores.

The great feature of the Ante-Nicene theology, even in the mistakes of the writers, is its reliance on the Holy Scripture. What wealth of Scripture they lavish in their pages! We identify the Scriptures by their aid; but, were they lost in other forms, we might almost restore them from their pages. And forever is the Church indebted to Origen for the patient and encyclopedic labor and learning which he bestowed on the Scriptures in producing his *Hexapla*. Would that, in his interpretations of the inspired text, he had more strictly adhered to the counsels of Leonides, who was of Bacon's opinion, that the meanings which flow naturally from the holy text are sweetest and best, even as that wine is best which is not crushed out and extorted from the grape, but which trickles of itself from the ripe and luscious cluster in all its purity and natural flavor. So Hooker remarks; and his view is commonly accepted by critics, that the interpretation of a text which departed most from its natural rendering is commonly the worst.

It is too striking an illustration of the childlike simplicity of the primitive faithful to be passed by, in Origen's history, that anecdote of his father, Leonides, who was himself a confessor and martyr: how he used to strip the bosom of his almost inspired boy as he lay asleep, and imprint kisses on his naked breast, "the temple of the Holy Ghost." That blessed Spirit, he believed, was near to his own lips when he thus saluted a Christian child, "for of such is the kingdom of heaven." From a child, this other Timothy "knew the Scriptures" indeed. His own doting father imbued him with the literature of the Greeks, but, far better, he taught him to love the lively oracles of the Lord of glory; and in these he became so proficient, even from tender years, that he puzzled his parent with his "understanding and answers," like the holy Child of Nazareth when He heard the doctors in the Temple, and also "asked them questions." In will he was also a martyr from his youth, and to the genuine spirit of martyrdom we must attribute that heroic fault of his youth which he lived to condemn in riper years, and which, evil and rash as it was, enabled the Church, once and for all, to give an authoritative interpretation to the language of the Savior, and to guard her children thenceforth from similar exploits of pious mistake. None can doubt the purity of the motive. Few draw the important inference of the nature of the Church's conflict with that intolerable prevalence of sensuality and shameless vice which so impressed her children with the import of Christ's words, "Blessed are the pure in heart: for they shall see God."

A Letter from Origen to Africanus

Here follows the very full account of the life of Origen by Dr. Crombie, professor of biblical criticism in St. Mary's College, St. Andrew:

Origen, surnamed Adamantinus, was born in all probability at Alexandria, about the year 185 a.d. Notwithstanding that his name is derived from that of an Egyptian deity, there seems no reason to doubt that his parents were Christian at the time of his birth. His father Leonides was probably, as has been conjectured, one of the many teachers of rhetoric or grammar who abounded in that city of Grecian culture, and appears to have been a man of decided piety. Under his superintendence, the youthful Origen was not only educated in the various branches of Grecian learning, but was also required daily to commit to memory and to repeat portions of Scripture prescribed him by his father; and while under this training, the spirit of inquiry into the meaning of Scripture, which afterwards formed so striking a feature in the literary character of the great Alexandrine, began to display itself. Eusebius relates that he was not satisfied with the plain and obvious meaning of the text, but sought to penetrate into its deeper signification, and caused his father trouble by the questions which he put to him regarding the sense of particular passages of Holy Writ. Leonides, like many parents, assumed the appearance of rebuking the curiosity of the boy for inquiring into things which were beyond his youthful capacity, and recommended him to be satisfied with the simple and apparent meaning of Scripture, while he is described as inwardly rejoicing at the signs of genius exhibited by his son, and as giving thanks to God for having made him the parent of such a child. But this state of things was not to last; for in the year 202 when Origen was about seventeen years of age, the great persecution of the Christians under Septimius Severus broke out, and among the victims was his father Leonides, who was apprehended and put in prison. Origen wished to share the fate of his father, but was prevented from quitting his home by the artifice of his mother, who was obliged to conceal his clothes to prevent him from carrying out his purpose. He wrote to his father, however, a letter, exhorting him to constancy under his trials, and entreating him not to change his convictions for the sake of his family. By the death of his father, whose property was confiscated to the imperial treasury, Origen was left, with his mother and six younger brothers dependent upon him for support. At this juncture, a wealthy and benevolent lady of Alexandria opened to him her house, of which he became an inmate for a short time. The society, however, which he found there was far from agreeable to the feelings of the youth. The lady had adopted as her son one Paul of Antioch, whom Eusebius terms an "advocate of the heretics then existing at Alexandria." The eloquence of the man drew crowds to hear him, although Origen could never be induced to regard him with any favor, nor even to join with him in any act of worship, giving then, as Eusebius remarks, "unmistakable specimens of the orthodoxy of his faith."

Finding his position in his household so uncomfortable, he resolved to enter upon the career of a teacher of grammar, and to support himself by his own exertions. As he had been carefully instructed by his father in Grecian literature, and had devoted himself to study after his death, he was enabled successfully to carry out his intention. And now begins the second stadium of his career.

The diligence and ability with which Origen prosecuted his profession speedily attracted attention and brought him many pupils. Among others who sought to avail themselves of his instructions in the principles of the Christian religion, were two young men, who afterwards became distinguished in the history of the Church, —Plutarch, who died the death of martyrdom, and Heraclas, who afterwards became bishop of Alexandria. It was not, however, merely by his success as a teacher that Origen gained a reputation. The brotherly kindness and unwearied affection which he displayed to all the victims of the persecution, which at that time was raging with peculiar severity at Alexandria under the prefect

A Letter from Origen to Africanus

Aquila, and in which many of his old pupils and friends were martyred, are described as being so marked and conspicuous, as to draw down upon him the fury of the mob, so that he was obliged on several occasions to flee from house to house to escape instant death. It is easy to understand that services of this kind could not fail to attract the attention of the heads of the Christian community at Alexandria; and partly, no doubt, because of these, but chiefly on account of his high literary reputation, Bishop Demetrius appointed him to the office of master in the Catechetical School, which was at that time vacant (by the departure of Clement, who had quitted the city on the outbreak of the persecution), although he was still a layman, and had not passed his eighteenth year. The choice of Demetrius was amply justified by the result. Origen discontinued his instructions in literature, in order to devote himself exclusively to the work of teaching in the Catechetical School. For his labors he refused all remuneration. He sold the books which he possessed, —many of them manuscripts which he himself had copied, —on condition of receiving from the purchaser four obols a day; and on this scanty pittance he subsisted, leading for many years a life of the greatest asceticism and devotion to study. After a day of labor in the school, he used to devote the greater part of the night to the investigation of Scripture, sleeping on the bare ground, and keeping frequent fasts. He carried out literally the command of the Savior, not to possess two coats, nor wear shoes. He consummated his work of mortification of the flesh by an act of self-mutilation, springing from a perverted interpretation of our Lord's words in Matthew xix. 12 and the desire to place himself beyond the reach of temptation in the intercourse which he necessarily had to hold with youthful female catechumens. This act was destined to exercise
a baneful influence upon his subsequent career in the Church.

During the episcopate of Zephyrinus (201–218) Origen visited Rome, and on his return again resumed his duties in the Catechetical School, transferring the care of the younger

Origen

catechumens to his friend and former pupil Heraclas, that he might devote himself with less distraction to the instruction of the more advanced, and to the more thorough investigation and exposition of Scripture. With a view to accomplish this more successfully, it is probable that about this time he set himself to acquire a knowledge of the Hebrew language, the fruit of which may be seen in the fragments which remain to us of his *magnum opus*, the *Hexapla*, and as many among the more cultured heathens, attracted by his reputation, seem to have attended his lectures, he felt it necessary to make himself more extensively acquainted with the doctrines of the Grecian schools, that he might meet his opponents upon their own ground, and for this purpose he attended the prelections of Ammonius Saccas, at that time in high repute at Alexandria as an expounder of the Neo-Platonic philosophy, of which school he has generally been considered the founder. The influence which the study of philosophical speculations exerted upon the mind of Origen may be traced in the whole course of his after development, and proved the fruitful source of many of those errors which were afterwards laid to his charge, and the controversies arising out of which disturbed the peace of the Church during the two following centuries. As was to be expected, the fame of the great Alexandrine teacher was not confined to his native city, but spread far and wide; and an evidence of this was the request made by the Roman governor of the province of Arabia to Demetrius and to the prefect of Egypt, that they would send Origen to him that he might hold an interview with one whose reputation was so great. We have no details of this visit, for all that Eusebius relates is that, "having accomplished the objects of his journey, he again returned to Alexandria." It was in the year 216 that the Emperor Caracalla visited Alexandria, and directed a bloody persecution against its inhabitants, especially the literary members of the community, in revenge for the sarcastic verses which had been composed against him for the murder of his brother Geta, a crime which he had perpetrated under circumstances of the basest treachery and cruelty.

Origen occupied too prominent a position in the literary Society of the city to be able to remain with safety, and therefore withdrew to Palestine to his friend Bishop Alexander of Jerusalem, and afterwards to Cæsarea, where he received an honorable welcome from Bishop Theoctistus. This step proved the beginning of his after troubles. These two men, filled with becoming admiration for the most learned teacher in the Church, requested him to expound the Scriptures in their presence in a public assembly of the Christians. Origen, although still a layman, and without any sacerdotal dignity in the Church, complied with the request. When this proceeding reached the ears of Demetrius, he was filled with the utmost indignation. "Such an act was never either heard or done before, that laymen should deliver discourses in the presence of the bishops," was his indignant remonstrance to the two offending bishops, and Origen received a command to return immediately to Alexandria. He obeyed, and for some years appears to have devoted himself solely to his studies in his usual spirit of self-abnegation.

It was probably during this period that the commencement of his friendship with Ambrosius is to be dated. Little is known of this individual. Eusebius states that he had formerly been an adherent of the Valentinian heresy, but had been converted by the arguments and eloquence of Origen to the orthodox faith of the Church. They became intimate friends; and as Ambrose seems to have been possessed of large means, and entertained an unbounded admiration of the learning and abilities of his friend, it was his delight to bear the expenses attending the transcription and publication of the many works which he persuaded him to give to the world. He furnished him "with more than seven amanuenses, who relieved each other at stated times, and with an equal number of transcribers, along with young girls who had been practiced in calligraphy," to make fair copies for publication of the works dictated by Origen. The literary activity of these years must have been prodigious, and probably they were among the happiest which Origen ever enjoyed. Engaged in his favorite studies, surrounded by many friends, adding yearly to his own stores of learning, and enriching the literature of the Church with treatises of the highest value in the department of sacred criticism and exegesis, it is difficult to conceive a condition of things more congenial to the mind of a true scholar. Only one incident of any importance seems to have taken place during these peaceful years, —his visit to Julia Mammæa, the pious mother of Alexander Severus. This noble lady had heard of the fame of Origen, and invited him to visit her at Antioch, sending a military escort to conduct him from Alexandria to the Syrian capital. He remained with her some time, "exhibiting innumerable illustrations of the glory of the Lord, and of the excellence of divine instruction, and then hastened back to his accustomed studies."

These happy years, however, were soon to end. Origen was called to Greece, probably about the year 228, upon what Eusebius vaguely calls "the pressing need of ecclesiastical affairs." But, this has generally been understood to refer to the prevalence of heretical views in the Church there, for the eradication of which the assistance of Origen was invoked. Before entering on this journey, he obtained letters of recommendation from his bishop. He passed through Palestine on his way to Greece, and at Cæsarea received at the hands of his friends Alexander and Theoctistus ordination to the office of presbyter, —an honor which proved to him afterwards the source of much persecution and annoyance. No doubt the motives of his friends were of the highest kind, and among them may have been the desire to take away the ground of objection formerly raised by Demetrius against the public preaching of a mere layman in the presence of a bishop. But they little dreamed of the storm which this act of theirs was to raise, and of the consequences which it was to bring upon the head of him whom they had sought to honor. After completing

his journey through Greece, Origen returned to Alexandria about the year 230. He there found his bishop greatly incensed against him for what had taken place at Cæsarea. Nor did his anger expend itself in mere objurgations and rebukes. In the year 231 a synod was summoned by Demetrius, composed of Egyptian bishops and Alexandrian presbyters, who declared Origen unworthy to hold the office of teacher, and excommunicated him from the fellowship of the Church of Alexandria. Even this did not satisfy the vindictive feeling of Demetrius. He summoned a second synod, in which the bishops alone were permitted to vote, and by their suffrages Origen was degraded from the office of presbyter, and intimation of this sentence was ordered to be made by encyclical letter to the various Churches. The validity of the sentence was recognized by all of them, with the exception of those in Palestine, Phoenicia, Arabia, and Achaia; a remarkable proof of the position of influence which was at that time held by the Church of Alexandria. Origen appears to have quitted the city before the bursting of the storm, and betook himself to Cæsarea, which henceforth became his home, and the seat of his labors for a period of nearly a quarter of a century. The motives which impelled Demetrius to this treatment of Origen have been variously stated and variously criticized. Eusebius refers his readers for a full account of all the matters involved
to the treatise which he and Pamphilus composed in his defense; but this work has not come down to us, although we possess a brief notice of it in the *Bibliotheca* of Photius, from which we derive our knowledge of the proceedings of the two synods. There seems little reason to doubt that jealousy of interference on the part of the bishops of another diocese was one main cause of the resentment displayed by Demetrius; while it is also possible that another alleged cause, the heterodox character of some of Origen's opinions, as made known in his already published works, among which were his *Stromata* and *De Principiis*, may have produced some effect upon the minds of the hostile bishops. Hefele asserts that the

act of the Palestinian bishops was contrary to the Church law of the time, and that Demetrius was justified on that ground for his procedure against him. But it may well be doubted whether there was any generally understood law or practice existing at so early a period of the Church's history. If so, it is difficult to understand how it should have been unknown to the Palestinian bishops; or, on the supposition of any such existing law or usage, it is equally difficult to conceive that either they themselves or Origen should have agreed to disregard it, knowing as they did the jealous temper of Demetrius, displayed on the occasion of Origen's preaching at Cæsarea already referred to. This had drawn from the Alexandrine bishop an indignant remonstrance, in which he had asserted that such an act was "quite unheard of before;" but, to this statement the Cæsarean bishops replied in a letter, in which they enumerated several instances of laymen who had addressed the congregation. The probabilities, therefore, are in favor of there being no generally understood law or practice on the subject, and that the procedure, therefore, was dictated by hierarchical jealousy on the part of Demetrius. According to Eusebius, indeed, the act of mutilation already referred to was made a ground of accusation against Origen; and there seems no doubt that there existed an old canon of the Church, based upon the words in Deuteronomy xxiii. 1, which rendered one who had committed such an act ineligible for office in the Church. But there is no trace of this act, as disqualifying Origen for the office of presbyter, having been urged by Demetrius, so far as can be discovered from the notices of the two synods which have been preserved by Rufinus and Photius. And it seems extremely probable, as Redepenning remarks, that if Demetrius were acquainted with this act of Origen, as Eusebius says he was, he made no public mention of it, far less that he made it a presence for his deposition.

      Demetrius did not long survive the execution of his vengeance against his unfortunate catechist. He died about a year afterwards, and was succeeded by Heraclas, the friend and former pupil of Origen. It does not, however, appear that Heraclas made any effort to have the sentence against Origen recalled, so that he might return to the early seat of his labors. Origen devoted himself at Cæsarea chiefly to exegetical studies upon the books of Scripture, enjoying the countenance and friendship of the two bishops Alexander and Theoctistus, who are said by Eusebius "to have attended him the whole time as pupils do their master." He speedily raised the theological school of that city to a degree of reputation which attracted many pupils. Among those who placed themselves under his instructions were two young Cappadocians, who had come to Cæsarea with other intentions, but who were so attracted by the whole character and personality of Origen, that they immediately became his pupils. The former of these, afterwards Gregory Thaumaturgus, Bishop of New Cæsarea, has left us, in the panegyric which he wrote after a discipleship of five years, a full and admiring account of the method of his great master.

The persecution under the Emperor Maximin obliged Origen to take refuge in Cæsarea in Cappadocia, where he remained in concealment about two years in the house of a Christian lady named Juliana, who was the heiress of Symmachus, the Ebionite translator of the Septuagint, and from whom he obtained several mss. which had belonged to Symmachus. Here, also, he composed his *Exhortation to Martyrdom*, which was expressly written for the sake of his friends Ambrosius and Protoctetus, who had been imprisoned on account of their Christian profession, but who recovered their freedom after the death of Maximin, —an event which allowed Origen to return to the Palestinian Cæsarea and to the prosecution of his labors. A visit to Athens, where he seems to have remained some time, and to Bostra in Arabia, in order to bring back to the true faith Bishop Beryllus, who had expressed heterodox opinions upon the subject of the divinity of Christ, (in which attempt he proved successful,) were the chief events of his life during the next five years. On the outbreak of the Decian persecution, however, in 249, he was imprisoned at Tyre, to which city he had gone from Cæsarea for some unknown reason, and was made to suffer great cruelties by his persecutors. The effect of these upon a frame worn out by ascetic labors may be easily conceived. Although he survived his imprisonment, his body was so weakened by his sufferings, that he died at Tyre in 254, in the seventieth year of his age.

The character of Origen is singularly pure and noble; for his moral qualities are as remarkable as his intellectual gifts. The history of the Church records the names of few whose patience and meekness under unmerited suffering were more conspicuous than his. How very differently would Jerome have acted under circumstances like those which led to Origen's banishment from Alexandria! And what a favorable contrast is presented by the self-denying asceticism of his whole life, to the sins which stained the early years of Augustine, prior to his conversion! The impression which his whole personality made upon those who came within the sphere of his influence is evidenced in a remarkable degree by the admiring affection displayed towards him by his friend Ambrose and his pupil Gregory. Nor was it friends alone that he so impressed. To him belongs the rare honor of convincing heretics of their errors, and of leading them back to the Church; a result which must have been due as much to the gentleness and earnestness of his Christian character, as to the prodigious learning, marvelous acuteness, and logical power, which entitle him to be regarded as the greatest of the Fathers. It is singular, indeed, that a charge of heresy should have been brought, not only after his death, but even during his life, against one who rendered such eminent services to the cause of orthodox Christianity. But this charge must be considered in reference to the times when he lived and wrote. No General Council had yet been held to settle authoritatively the doctrine of the Church upon any of those great questions, the discussion of which convulsed the Christian world during the two following

centuries; and in these circumstances greater latitude was naturally permissible than would have been justifiable at a later period. Moreover, a mind so speculative as that of Origen, and so engrossed with the deepest and most difficult problems of human thought, must sometimes have expressed itself in a way liable to be misunderstood. But no doubt the chief cause of
his being regarded as a heretic is to be found in the haste with which he allowed many of his writings to be published. Had he considered more carefully what he intended to bring before the public eye, less occasion would have been furnished to objectors, and the memory of one of the greatest scholars and most devoted Christians that the world has ever seen
would have been freed, to a great extent at least, from the reproach of heresy.

Origen was a very voluminous author. Jerome says that he wrote more than any individual could read; and Epiphanius relates that his writings amounted to 6,000 volumes, by which statement we are probably to understand that every individual treatise, large or small, including each of the numerous homilies, was counted as a separate volume. The admiration entertained for him by his friend Ambrosius, and the readiness with which the latter bore all the expenses of transcription and publication, led Origen to give to the world much which otherwise would never have seen the light.

The works of the great Adamantinus may be classed under the following divisions:

(1) Exegetical Works.

These comprise Σχόλια, brief notes on Scripture, of which only fragments remain: Τόμοι, Commentaries, lengthened expositions, of which we possess considerable portions,
including those on Matthew, John, and Epistle to the Romans; and about 200 Homilies, upon the principal books of the Old and New Testaments, a full list of which may be seen in

Migne's edition. In these works, his peculiar system of interpretation found ample scope for exercise; and although he carried out his principle of allegorizing many things, which in their historical and literal signification offended his exegetical sense, he nevertheless maintains that "the passages which hold good in their historical acceptation are much more numerous than those which contain a purely spiritual meaning." The student will find much that is striking and suggestive in his remarks upon the various passages which he brings under review. For an account of his method of interpreting Scripture, and the grounds on which he based it, the reader may consult the fourth book of the treatise *On the Principles*.

(2) Critical Works.

The great critical work of Origen was the *Hexapla* or Six-columned Bible; an attempt to provide a revised text of the Septuagint translation of Old Testament Scripture. On this undertaking he is said to have spent eight-and-twenty years of his life, and to have acquired a knowledge of Hebrew in order to qualify himself for the task. Each page of this work consisted, with the exception to be noticed immediately, of six columns. In the first was placed the current Hebrew text; in the second, the same represented in *Greek* letters; in the third, the version of Aquila; in the fourth, that of Symmachus; in the fifth, the text of the LXX., as it existed at the time; and in the sixth, the version of Theodotion. Having come into possession also of certain other Greek translations of some of the books of Scripture, he added these in their appropriate place, so that the work presented in some parts the appearance of seven, eight, or nine columns, and was termed Heptapla, Octopla, or Enneapla, in consequence. He inserted critical marks in the text of the LXX., an asterisk to denote what ought to be added, and an obelus to denote what ought to be omitted; taking the additions chiefly from the version of Theodotion. The work, with the omission of the Hebrew column, and that representing the Hebrew in Greek letters, was termed Tetrapla; and with regard to it, it is uncertain whether it is to be considered a preliminary work on the part of Origen, undertaken by way of preparation for the larger, or merely as an excerpt from the latter. The whole extended, it is said, to nearly fifty volumes, and was, of course, far too bulky for common use, and too costly for transcription. It was placed in some repository in the city of Tyre, from which it was removed after Origen's death to the library at Cæsarea, founded by Pamphilus, the friend of Eusebius. It is supposed to have been burnt at the capture of Cæsarea by the Arabs in 653 a.d. The column, however, containing the version of the LXX. had been copied by Pamphilus and Eusebius, along with the critical marks of Origen, although, owing to carelessness on the part of subsequent transcribers, the text was soon again corrupted. The remains of this work were published by Montfaucon at Paris, 1713, 2 vols. folio; by Bahrdt at Leipsic in 1769; and is at present again in course of publication from the Clarendon press, Oxford, under the editorship of Mr. Field, who has made use of the Syriac-Hexaplar version, and has added various fragments not contained in prior editions. (For a full and critical account of this work, the English reader is referred to Dr. Sam. Davidson's *Biblical Criticism*, vol. i. ch. xii., which has been made use of for the above notice.)

(3) Apologetical Works.

His great apologetical work was the treatise undertaken at the special request of his friend Ambrosius, in answer to the attack of the heathen philosopher Celsus on the Christian religion, in a work which he entitled Λόγος ἀληθής or *A True Discourse*. Origen states that he had heard that there were two individuals of this name, both of them Epicureans, the earlier of the two having lived in the time of Nero, and the other in the

time of Adrian, or later. Redepenning is of opinion that Celsus must have composed his work in the time of Marcus Aurelius (161–180 a.d.), on account of his supposed mention of the Marcionites (whose leader did not make his appearance at Rome before 142 a.d.), and of the Marcellians (followers of the Carpocratian Marcellina), a sect which was founded after the year 155 a.d. under Bishop Anicetus. Origen believed his opponent to be an Epicurean, but to have adopted other doctrines than those of Epicurus, because he thought that by so doing he could assail Christianity to greater advantage. The work which Origen composed in answer to the so-styled *True Discourse* consists of eight books, and belongs to the latest years of his life. It has always been regarded as the great apologetic work of antiquity; and no one can peruse it without being struck by the multifarious reading, wonderful acuteness, and rare subtlety of mind which it displays. But the rule which Origen prescribed to himself, of not allowing a single objection of his opponent to remain unanswered, leads him into a
minuteness of detail, and into numerous repetitions, which fatigue the reader, and detract from the interest and unity of the work. He himself confesses that he began it on one plan,
and carried it out on another. No doubt, had he lived to re-write and condense it, it would have been more worthy of his reputation. But with all its defects, it is a great work, and well deserves the notice of the students of Apologetics. The table of contents subjoined to the translation will convey a better idea of its nature than any description which our limits would permit us to give.

(4) Dogmatic Works.

These include the Στρωματεῖς, a work composed in imitation of the treatise of Clement of the same name, and consisting originally of ten books, of which only three fragments exist in a Latin version by Jerome; a treatise on the

Resurrection, of which four fragments remain; and the treatise Περὶ 'Αρχῶν, *De Principiis*, which contains Origen's views on various questions of systematic theology. The work has come down to us in the Latin translation of his admirer Rufinus; but, from a comparison of the few fragments of the original Greek which have been preserved, we see that Rufinus was justly chargeable with altering many of Origen's expressions, in order to bring his doctrine on certain points more into harmony with the orthodox views of the time. The *De Principiis* consists of four books, and is the first of the works of Origen in this series, to which we refer the reader.

(5) Practical Works.

Under this head we place the little treatise Περὶ Εὐχῆς, *On Prayer*, written at the instance of his friend Ambrose, and which contains an exposition of the Lord's Prayer; the Λόγος προτρεπτικὸς εἰς μαρτύριον, *Exhortation to Martyrdom*, composed at the outbreak of the persecution by Maximian, when his friends Ambrose and Protoctetus were imprisoned. Of his numerous letters only two have come down entire, viz., that which was addressed to Julius Africanus, who had questioned the genuineness of the history of Susanna in the apocryphal additions to the book of Daniel, and that to Gregory Thaumaturgus on the use of Greek philosophy in the explanation of Scripture, although, from the brevity of the latter, it is questionable whether it is more than a fragment of the original. The Φιλοκαλία, *Philocalia*, was a compilation from the writings of Origen, intended to explain the difficult passages of Scripture, and executed by Basil the Great and Gregory of Nazianzum; large extracts of which have been preserved, especially of that part which was taken from the treatise against Celsus. The remains were first printed at Paris in 1618, and again at Cambridge in 1676, in the reprint of Spencer's edition of the *Contra Celsum*. In the Benedictine edition, and in Migne's reprint, the various portions are quoted in footnotes under the respective passages of Origen's writings.

(6) Editions of Origin.

The first published works of Origen were his Homilies, which appeared in 1475, although neither the name of the publisher nor the place of publication is given. These were followed by the treatise against Celsus in the translation of Christopher Persana, which appeared at Rome in 1481; and this, again, by an edition of the Homilies at Venice in 1503, containing those on the first four books of Moses, Joshua, and Judges. The first collective edition of the whole works was given to the world in a Latin translation by James Merlin, and was published in two folio volumes, first at Paris in 1512 and 1519, and afterwards at Paris in 1522 and 1530. A revision of Merlin's edition was begun by Erasmus, and completed, after his death, by Beatus Rhenanus. This appeared at Basle in 1536 in two folio volumes, and again in 1557 and 1571. A much better and more complete edition was undertaken by the Benedictine Gilbertus Genebrardus, which was published also in two volumes folio at Paris in 1574, and again in 1604 and 1619. Hoeschel published the treatise against Celsus at Augsburg in 1605; Spencer, at Cambridge in 1658 and 1677, to which was added the *Philocalia*, which had first appeared in a Latin translation by Genebrardus, and afterwards in Greek by Tarinus at Paris in 1618 and 1624, in quarto. Huet, Bishop of Avranches, published the exegetical writings in Greek, including the Commentaries on Matthew and John, in two volumes folio, of which the one appeared at Rouen in 1668, and the other at Paris in 1679. The great edition by the two learned Benedictines of St. Maur—Charles de la Rue, and his nephew Vincent de la Rue—was published at Paris between the years 1733 and 1759. This is a work of immense industry and labor, and remains the standard to the present time. It has been reprinted by Migne in his series of the Greek Fathers, in nine volumes, large 8vo. In Oberthür's series of the Greek Fathers, seven volumes contain the chief portion of Origen's writings; while Lommatzsch has published the whole in twenty-five small volumes, Berlin, 1831–48, containing the Greek text alone.

For further information upon the life and opinions of Origen, the reader may consult Redepenning's *Origenes*, 2 vols., Bonn, 1841, 1846; the articles in Herzog's *Encyclopädie* and Wetzer's and Wette's *Kirchen-Lexikon*, by Kling and Hefele respectively; the brilliant sketch by Pressensé in his *Martyrs and Apologists*; and the learned compilation of Huet, entitled *Origeniana*, to be found in the ninth volume of Migne's edition.

[In the Edinburgh series the foregoing Life was delayed till the appearance of the second volume. The earlier volume appeared with a preface, as follows:]—

The name of the illustrious Origen comes before us in this series in connection with his works *De Principiis, Epistola ad Africanum, Epistola ad Gregorium*, and the treatise *Contra Celsum*.

It is in his treatise Περὶ Ἀρχῶν, or, as it is commonly known under the Latin title, *De Principiis*, that most fully develops his system, and brings out his peculiar principles. None of his works exposed him to so much animadversion in the ancient Church as this. On it chiefly was based the charge of heresy which some vehemently pressed against him, —a charge from which even his firmest friends felt it no easy matter absolutely to defend him. The points on which it was held that he had plainly departed from the orthodox faith, were the four following: *First*, That the souls of men had existed in a previous state, and that their imprisonment in material bodies was a punishment for sins which they had then committed. *Second*, That the human soul of Christ had also previously existed, and been united to the Divine nature before that incarnation of the Son of God which is related in the Gospels.

Third, that our material bodies shall be transformed into absolutely ethereal ones at the resurrection; and *Fourth*, that all men, and even devils, shall be finally restored through the mediation of Christ. His principles of interpreting Scripture are also brought out in this treatise; and while not a little ingenuity is displayed in illustrating and maintaining them, the serious errors into which they might too easily lead will be at once perceived by the reader.

It is much to be regretted that the original Greek of the *De Principiis* has for the most part perished. We possess it chiefly in a Latin translation by Rufinus. And there can be no doubt that he often took great liberties with his author. So much was this felt to be the case, that Jerome undertook a new translation of the work; but only small portions of his version have reached our day. He strongly accuses Rufinus of unfaithfulness as an interpreter, while he also inveighs bitterly against Origen himself, as having departed from the Catholic Faith, especially in regard to the doctrine of the Trinity. There seems, however, after all, no adequate reason to doubt the substantial orthodoxy of our author, although the bent of his mind and the nature of his studies led him to indulge in many vain and unauthorized speculations.

The *Epistle to Africanus* was drawn forth by a letter which that learned writer had addressed to Origen respecting the story of Susanna appended to the book of Daniel. Africanus had grave doubts as to the canonical authority of the account. Origen replies to his objections, and seeks to uphold the story as both useful in itself, and a genuine portion of the ancient prophetical writings.

The treatise of Origen *Against Celsus* is, of all his works, the most interesting to the modern reader. It is a defense of Christianity in opposition to a Greek philosopher named Celsus, who had attacked it in a work entitled ’Αληθὴς Λόγος, that is, *The True Word*, or *The True Discourse*. Of this work we know nothing, except from the quotations contained in the answer given to it by Origen. Nor has anything very certain been ascertained respecting its author. According to Origen, he was a follower of Epicures, but others have regarded him as a Platonist. If we may judge of the work by those specimens of it presented in the reply of Origen, it was little better than a compound of sophistry and slander. But there is reason to be grateful for it, as having called forth the admirable answer of Origen. This work was written in the old age of our author, and is composed with great care; while it abounds with proofs of the widest erudition. It is also perfectly orthodox; and, as Bishop Bull has remarked, it is only fair that we should judge from a work written with the view of being considered by the world at large, and with the most elaborate care, as to the mature and finally accepted views of the author.

The best edition of Origen's works is that superintended by Charles and Charles Vincent de la Rue, Paris, 1783, 4 vols. fol., which is reprinted by Migne. There is also an edition in 25 volumes, based upon that of De la Rue, but without the Latin translation, by Lommatzsch, Berlin, 1831–1848. The *De Principiis* has been separately edited by Redepenning, Leipzig, 1836. Spencer edited the *Contra Celsum*, Cambridge, 1677.

[Professor Crombie was assisted in the *Contra Celsum* by the Rev. W. H. Cairns, M.A., Rector of the Dumfries Academy. Mr. Cairns (since deceased) was the translator of Books VII. and VIII. of that work.]

[The Works of Origen included in this volume having been placed in my hands by the Right Reverend Editor of the present series (who restricts himself to a limited task of supervision), I have endeavored to do for them that which seemed needful in the circumstances. The temptation was strong to enter upon annotations, for which no one of the authors among the Ante-Nicene Fathers offers larger room, and to insert corrections of various sorts, based upon modern progress and research. But, in accordance with the plan of this series, I have been forced to resist this temptation, and have striven only to be useful in matters which, though of great moment, are toilsome, and in no wise flattering to editorial vanity or conceit.

I have silently corrected numerous typographical errors which exist in the Edinburgh edition, and have sought to secure uniformity in the details of reproducing the work, and, above all, accuracy in all its parts. Particularly, I may mention that the Scripture references needed correction to the extent of more than a hundred places, and that references to classical and other writers were often quite astray. A very few notes, enclosed in brackets, are all that I have deemed it expedient or proper, on my part, to add.

While no one who is aware of human infirmity will ever dare to claim perfection in the typography of a book which has passed through the press under his hands, yet in the present case I venture to assure the student and reader that no pains or effort have been spared in order to make the volume as accurate as possible in this respect. Much experience and training incline me to hope and believe that success has attended my efforts. S.]

Prefatory Notice to Origen's Works.

[The great biblical scholar and critic of the first half of the third century deserves a more cordial recognition and appreciation than have always been accorded to him. While it is true that in various matters he has strange, even wild, fancies, and gives utterance to expressions which can hardly, if at all, be justified; while it is also true that he indulges beyond all reason (as it appears to us of the present age) in utterly useless speculations, and carries to excess his great love of allegorizing,—yet these are rather of the nature of possible guesses and surmises on numerous topics, of more or less interest, than deliberate, systematic teaching as matters of faith. He frequently speaks of them in this wise, and does not claim for these guesses and speculations any more credit than they may appear to his readers to be worth. In the great fundamentals of the Christian creed Origen is unquestionably sound and true. He does not always express himself in accordance with the exact definitions which the Church Catholic secured in the century after his decease, as a necessary result of the struggle with Arian and other deadly heresies; but surely, in fairness, he is not to be too severely judged for this. Some writers (e.g., J. M. Neale, in his *History of the Patriarchate of Alexandria*) give an unfavorable and condemnatory view of Origen and his career, but I am of opinion that Neale and others push their objections much too far. I hold that Bishop Bull, and men like him, are nearer to truth and justice in defending Origen and his lifelong labors in the cause of the Master.

The Περὶ Ἀρχῶν, which has come to us through the professedly paraphrastic but really unsatisfactory version of Rufinus, is the work which has given chief offence, and brought much odium upon Origen; but as this was written in early life, and it is doubtful in how far Origen is responsible for many things that are in it, it is only fair and just to judge him by such works as the Κατὰ Κέλσον and his valuable *Homilies* on various books of Holy Scripture. These go far to prove clearly that he, whom Dr. Barrow designates as "the father of interpreters," is worthy the high estimate which ancient as well as modern defenders of his good name have fully set forth, and to justify the conviction, that, if we possessed more out of the numerous works of his which have entirely perished, we should rank him even more highly than is done by Bishop Bull in his *Defensio Fidei Nicenæ*.

In conclusion, I give a paragraph from the very valuable *Introduction to the Criticism of the New Testament*, by Dr. F. H. Scrivener, one of the ablest of living biblical scholars and critics: —

"Origen is the most celebrated biblical critic of antiquity. His is the highest name among the critics and expositors of the early Church. He is perpetually engaged in the discussion of various readings of the New Testament, and employs language, in describing the then existing state of the text, which would be deemed strong if applied even to its present condition, after the changes which sixteen more centuries must needs have produced....Seldom have such warmth of fancy and so bold a grasp of mind been united with the lifelong, patient industry which procured for this famous man the honorable appellation of *Adamantius*." S.]

Prologue of Rufinus.

I know that very many of the brethren, induced by their thirst for a knowledge of the Scriptures, have requested some distinguished men, well versed in Greek learning, to translate Origen into Latin, and so make him accessible to Roman readers. Among these, when our brother and colleague had, at the earnest entreaty of Bishop Damasus, translated two of the Homilies on the Song of Songs out of Greek into Latin, he prefixed so elegant and noble a preface to that work, as to inspire every one with a most eager desire to read and study Origen, saying that the expression, "The King hath brought me into his chamber," was appropriate to his feelings, and declaring that while Origen in his other works surpassed all writers, he in the Song of Songs surpassed even himself. He promises, indeed, in that very preface, that he will present the books on the Song of Songs, and numerous others of the works of Origen, in a Latin translation, to Roman readers. But he, finding greater pleasure in compositions of his own, pursues an end that is attended with greater fame, viz., in being the author rather than the translator of works. Accordingly, we enter upon the undertaking, which was thus begun and approved of by

A Letter from Origen to Africanus

him, although we cannot compose in a style of elegance equal to that of a man of such distinguished eloquence; and
therefore, I am afraid lest, through my fault, the result should follow, that that man, whom he deservedly esteems as the second teacher of knowledge and wisdom in the Church after the apostles, should, through the poverty of my language, appear far inferior to what he is. And this consideration, which frequently recurred to my mind, kept me silent, and prevented me from yielding to the numerous entreaties of my brethren, until your influence, my very faithful brother Macarius, which is so great, rendered it impossible for my unskillfulness any longer to offer resistance. And therefore, that I might not find you too grievous an exactor, I gave way, even contrary to my resolution; on the condition and arrangement, however, that in my translation I should follow as far as possible the rule observed by my predecessors, and especially by that distinguished man whom I have mentioned above, who, after translating into Latin more than seventy of those treatises of Origen which are styled *Homilies* and a considerable number also of his writings on the apostles, in which a good many "stumbling-blocks" are found in the original Greek, so smoothed and corrected them in his translation, that a Latin reader would meet with nothing which could appear discordant with our belief. His example, therefore, we follow, to the best of our ability; if not with equal power of eloquence, yet at least with the same strictness of rule, taking care not to reproduce those expressions occurring in the works of Origen which are inconsistent with and opposed to each other. The cause of these variations we have explained more freely in the *Apologeticus*,
which Pamphilus wrote in defense of the works of Origen, where we added a brief tract, in which we showed, I think, by unmistakable proofs, that his books had been corrupted
in numerous places by heretics and malevolent persons, and especially those books of which you now require me to undertake the translation, i.e., the books which may be entitled *De Principiis* or *De Principatibus*, and which are indeed in

other respects full of obscurities and difficulties. For he there discusses those subjects with respect to which philosophers, after spending all their lives upon them, have been unable to discover anything. But here our author strove, as much as in him lay, to turn to the service of religion the belief in a Creator, and the rational nature of created beings, which the latter had degraded to purposes of wickedness. If, therefore, we have found anywhere in his writings, any statement opposed to that view, which elsewhere in his works he had himself piously laid down regarding the Trinity, we have either omitted it, as being corrupt, and not the composition of Origen, or we have brought it forward agreeably to the rule which we frequently find affirmed by himself. If, indeed, in his desire to pass rapidly on, he has, as speaking to persons of skill and knowledge, sometimes expressed himself obscurely, we have, in order that the passage might be clearer, added what we had read more fully stated on the same subject in his other works, keeping explanation in view, but adding nothing of our own, but simply restoring to him what was his, although occurring in other portions of his writings.

These remarks, therefore, by way of admonition, I have made in the preface, lest slanderous individuals perhaps should think that they had a second time discovered matter of accusation. But let perverse and disputatious men have a care what they are about. For we have in the meantime undertaken this heavy labor, if God should aid your prayers, not to shut the mouths of slanderers (which is impossible, although God perhaps will do it), but to afford material to those who desire to advance in the knowledge of these things. And, verily, in the presence of God the Father, and of the Son, and of the Holy Spirit, I adjure and beseech everyone, who may either transcribe or read these books, by his belief in the kingdom to come, by the mystery of the resurrection from the dead, and by that everlasting fire prepared for the devil and his angels, that, as he would not possess for an eternal inheritance that place where there is weeping and gnashing of teeth, and where their

A Letter from Origen to Africanus

fire is not quenched and their worm dieth not, he add nothing to Scripture, and take nothing away from it, and make no insertion or alteration, but that he compare his transcript with the copies from which he made it, and make the emendations and distinctions according to the letter, and not have his manuscript incorrect or indistinct, lest the difficulty of ascertaining the sense, from the indistinctness of the copy, should cause greater difficulties to the readers.

A Letter to Origen from Africanus About the History of Susanna.

Greeting, my lord and son, most worthy Origen, from Africanus. In your sacred discussion with Agnomon you referred to that prophecy of Daniel which is related of his youth. This at that time, as was meet, I accepted as genuine. Now, however, I cannot understand how it escaped you that this part of the book is spurious. For, in sooth, this section, although apart from this it is elegantly written, is plainly a more modern forgery. There are many proofs of this. When Susanna is condemned to die, the prophet is seized by the Spirit, and cries out that the sentence is unjust. Now, in the first place, it is always in some other way that Daniel prophesies— by visions, and dreams, and an angel appearing to him, never by prophetic inspiration. Then, after crying out in this extraordinary fashion, he detects them in a way no less incredible, which not even Philistion the play-writer would have resorted to. For, not satisfied with rebuking them through the Spirit, he placed them apart, and asked them severally where they saw her committing adultery. And when the one said, "Under a holm-tree" (*prinos*), he answered that the angel would saw him asunder (*prisein*); and in a similar fashion menaced the other who said, "Under a mastich-tree" (*schinos*), with being rent asunder (*schisthenai*). Now, in Greek, it happens that "holm-tree" and "saw asunder," and "rend" and "mastich-tree" sound alike; but in Hebrew they are quite distinct. But all the books of the Old Testament have been translated from Hebrew into Greek.

2. Moreover, how is it that they who were captives among the Chaldæans, lost and won at play, thrown out unburied on the streets, as was prophesied of the former captivity, their sons torn from them to be eunuchs, and their daughters to be concubines, as had been prophesied; how is it that such could pass sentence of death, and that on the wife of their king Joakim, whom the king of the Babylonians had made partner of his throne? Then if it was not this Joakim, but some other from the common people, whence had a captive such a mansion and spacious garden? But a more fatal objection is, that this section, along with the other two at the end of it, is not contained in the Daniel received among the Jews. And add that, among all the many prophets who had been before, there is no one who has quoted from another word for word. For they had no need to go a-begging for words, since their own were true; but this one, in rebuking one of those men, quotes the words of the Lord: "The innocent and righteous shalt thou not slay." From all this I infer that this section is a later addition. Moreover, the style is different. I have struck the blow; do you give the echo; answer, and instruct me. Salute all my masters. The learned all salute thee. With all my heart I pray for your and your circle's health.

A Letter from Origen to Africanus.

Origen to Africanus, a beloved brother in God the Father, through Jesus Christ, His holy Child, greeting. Your letter, from which I learn what you think of the Susanna in the Book of Daniel, which is used in the Churches, although apparently somewhat short, presents in its few words many problems, each of which demands no common treatment, but such as oversteps the character of a letter, and reaches the limits of a discourse. And I, when I consider, as best I can, the measure of my intellect, that I may know myself, am aware that I am wanting in the accuracy necessary to reply to your letter; and that the more, that the few days I have spent in Nicomedia have been far from sufficient to send you an answer to all your demands and queries even after the fashion of the present epistle. Wherefore pardon my little ability, and the little time I had, and read this letter with all indulgence, supplying anything I may omit.

2. You begin by saying, that when, in my discussion with our friend Bassus, I used the Scripture which contains the prophecy of Daniel when yet a young man in the affair of Susanna, I did this as if it had escaped me that this part of the book was spurious. You say that you praise this passage as elegantly written, but find fault with it as a more modern composition, and a forgery; and you add that the forger has had recourse to something which not even Philistion the play-writer would have used in his puns between *prinos* and *prisein*, *schinos* and *schisis*, which words as they sound in Greek can be used in this way, but not in Hebrew. In answer to this, I have to tell you what it behooves us to do in the cases not only of the History of Susanna, which is found in every Church of Christ in that Greek copy which the Greeks use, but is not in the Hebrew, or of the two other passages you mention at the end of the book containing the history of Bel and the Dragon, which likewise are not in the Hebrew copy of Daniel; but of thousands of other passages also which I found in many places when with my little strength I was collating the Hebrew copies with ours. For in Daniel itself I found the word "bound" followed in our versions by very many verses which are not in the Hebrew at all, beginning (according to one of the copies which circulate in the Churches) thus: "Ananias, and Azarias, and Misael prayed and sang unto God," down to "O, all ye that worship the Lord, bless ye the God of gods. Praise Him, and say that His mercy endures for ever and ever. And it came to pass, when the king heard them singing, and saw them that they

were alive." Or, as in another copy, from "And they walked in the midst of the fire, praising God and blessing the Lord," down to "O, all ye that worship the Lord, bless ye the God of gods. Praise Him, and say that His mercy endures to all generations." But in the Hebrew copies the words, "And these three men, Sedrach, Misach, and Abednego fell down bound into the midst of the fire," are immediately followed by the verse, "Nabouchodonosor the king was astonished, and rose up in haste, and spoke, and said unto his counsellors." For so Aquila, following the Hebrew reading, gives it, who has obtained the credit among the Jews of having interpreted the Scriptures with no ordinary care, and whose version is most commonly used by those who do not know Hebrew, as the one which has been most successful. Of the copies in my possession whose readings I gave, one follows the Seventy, and the other Theodotion; and just as the History of Susanna which you call a forgery is found in both, together with the passages at the end of Daniel, so they give also these passages, amounting, to make a rough guess, to more than two hundred verses.

3. And in many other of the sacred books I found sometimes more in our copies than in the Hebrew, sometimes less. I shall adduce a few examples, since it is impossible to give them all. Of the Book of Esther neither the prayer of Mardochaios nor that of Esther, both fitted to edify the reader, is found in the Hebrew. Neither are the letters; nor the one written to Amman about the rooting up of the Jewish nation, nor that of Mardochaios in the name of Artaxerxes delivering the nation from death. Then in Job, the words from "It is written, that he shall rise again with those whom the Lord raises," to the end, are not in the Hebrew, and so not in Aquila's edition; while they are found in the Septuagint and in Theodotion's version, agreeing with each other at least in sense. And many other places I found in Job where our copies have more than the Hebrew ones, sometimes a little more,

and sometimes a great deal more: a little more, as when to the words, "Rising up in the morning, he offered burnt-offerings for them according to their number," they add, "one heifer for the sin of their soul;" and to the words, "The angels of God came to present themselves before God, and the devil came with them," "from going to and fro in the earth, and from walking up and down in it." Again, after "The Lord gave, the Lord has taken away," the Hebrew has not, "It was so, as seemed good to the Lord." Then our copies are very much fuller than the Hebrew, when Job's wife speaks to him, from "How long wilt thou hold out? And he said, Lo, I wait yet a little while, looking for the hope of my salvation," down to "that I may cease from my troubles, and my sorrows which compass me." For they have only these words of the woman, "But say a word against God, and die."

4. Again, through the whole of Job there are many passages in the Hebrew which are wanting in our copies, generally four or five verses, but sometimes, however, even fourteen, and nineteen, and sixteen. But why should I enumerate all the instances I collected with so much labor, to prove that the difference between our copies and those of the Jews did not escape me? In Jeremiah I noticed many instances, and indeed in that book I found much transposition and variation in the readings of the prophecies. Again, in Genesis, the words, "God saw that it was good," when the firmament was made, are not found in the Hebrew, and there is no small dispute among them about this; and other instances are to be found in Genesis, which I marked, for the sake of distinction, with the sign the Greeks call an obelisk, as on the other hand I marked with an asterisk those passages in our copies which are not found in the Hebrew. What needs there to speak of Exodus, where there is such diversity in what is said about the tabernacle and its court, and the ark, and the garments of the high priest and the priests, that sometimes the meaning even does not seem to be akin? And, forsooth, when we notice such things, we are forthwith to reject as spurious the copies in use

in our Churches, and enjoin the brotherhood to put away the sacred books current among them, and to coax the Jews, and persuade them to give us copies which shall be untampered with, and free from forgery! Are we to suppose that that Providence which in the sacred Scriptures has ministered to the edification of all the Churches of Christ, had no thought for those bought with a price, for whom Christ died; whom, although His Son, God who is love spared not, but gave Him up for us all, that with Him He might freely give us all things?

5. In all these cases consider whether it would not be well to remember the words, "Thou shalt not remove the ancient landmarks which thy fathers have set." Nor do I say this because I shun the labor of investigating the Jewish Scriptures, and comparing them with ours, and noticing their various readings. This, if it be not arrogant to say it, I have already to a great extent done to the best of my ability, laboring hard to get at the meaning in all the editions and various readings; while I paid particular attention to the interpretation of the Seventy, lest I might to be found to accredit any forgery to the Churches which are under heaven, and give an occasion to those who seek such a starting-point for gratifying their desire to slander the common brethren, and to bring some accusation against those who shine forth in our community. And I make it my endeavor not to be ignorant of their various readings, lest in my controversies with the Jews I should quote to them what is not found in their copies, and that I may make some use of what is found there, even although it should not be in our Scriptures. For if we are so prepared for them in our discussions, they will not, as is their manner, scornfully laugh at Gentile believers for their ignorance of the true reading as they have them. So far as to the History of Susanna not being found in the Hebrew.

6. Let us now look at the things you find fault with in the story itself. And here let us begin with what would probably make any one averse to receiving the history: I mean the play of words between *prinos* and *prisis*, *schinos* and

schisis. You say that you can see how this can be in Greek, but that in Hebrew the words are altogether distinct. On this point, however, I am still in doubt; because, when I was considering this passage (for I myself saw this difficulty), I consulted not a few Jews about it, asking them the Hebrew words for *prinos* and *prisein,* and how they would translate *schinos* the tree, and how *schisis.* And they said that they did not know these Greek words *prinos* and *schinos,* and asked me to show them the trees, that they might see what they called them. And I at once (for the truth's dear sake) put before them pieces of the different trees. One of them then said, that he could not with any certainty give the Hebrew name of anything not mentioned in Scripture, since, if one was at a loss, he was prone to use the Syriac word instead of the Hebrew one; and he went on to say, that some words the very wisest could not translate. "If, then," said he, "you can adduce a passage in any Scripture where the *schinos* is mentioned, or the *prinos,* you will find there the words you seek, together with the words which have the same sound; but if it is nowhere mentioned, we also do not know it." This, then, being what the Hebrews said to whom I had recourse, and who were acquainted with the history, I am cautious of affirming whether or not there is any correspondence to this play of words in the Hebrew. Your reason for affirming that there is not, you yourself probably know.

7. Moreover, I remember hearing from a learned Hebrew, said among themselves to be the son of a wise man, and to have been specially trained to succeed his father, with whom I had intercourse on many subjects, the names of these elders, just as if he did not reject the History of Susanna, as they occur in Jeremias as follows: "The Lord make thee like Zedekias and Achiab, whom the king of Babylon roasted in the fire, for the iniquity they did in Israel." How, then, could the one be sawn asunder by an angel, and the other rent in pieces? The answer is, that these things were prophesied not of this world, but of the judgment of God, after the departure from this

world. For as the lord of that wicked servant who says, "My lord delayeth his coming," and so gives himself up to drunkenness, eating and drinking with drunkards, and smiting his fellow-servants, shall at his coming "cut him asunder, and appoint him his portion with the unbelievers," even so the angels appointed to punish will accomplish these things (just as they will cut asunder the wicked steward of that passage) on these men, who were called indeed elders, but who administered their stewardship wickedly. One will saw asunder him who was waxen old in wicked days, who had pronounced false judgment, condemning the innocent, and letting the guilty go free; and another will rend in pieces him of the seed of Chanaan, and not of Judah, whom beauty had deceived, and whose heart lust had perverted.

8. And I knew another Hebrew, who told about these elders such traditions as the following: that they pretended to the Jews in captivity, who were hoping by the coming of Christ to be freed from the yoke of their enemies, that they could explain clearly the things concerning Christ,...and that they so deceived the wives of their countrymen. Wherefore it is that the prophet Daniel calls the one "waxen old in wicked days," and says to the other, "Thus have ye dealt with the children of Israel; but the daughters of Juda would not abide your wickedness."

9. But probably to this you will say, Why then is the "History" not in their Daniel, if, as you say, their wise men hand down by tradition such stories? The answer is, that they hid from the knowledge of the people as many of the passages which contained any scandal against the elders, rulers, and judges, as they could, some of which have been preserved in uncanonical writings (Apocrypha). As an example, take the story told about Esaias; and guaranteed by the Epistle to the Hebrews, which is found in none of their public books. For the author of the Epistle to the Hebrews, in speaking of the prophets, and what they suffered, says, "They were stoned, they were sawn asunder, they were slain with the sword." To

whom, I ask, does the "sawn asunder" refer (for by an old idiom, not peculiar to Hebrew, but found also in Greek, this is said in the plural, although it refers to but one person)? Now we know very well that tradition says that Esaias the prophet was sawn asunder; and this is found in some apocryphal work, which probably the Jews have purposely tampered with, introducing some phrases manifestly incorrect, that discredit might be thrown on the whole.

However, someone hard pressed by this argument may have recourse to the opinion of those who reject this Epistle as not being Paul's; against whom I must at some other time use other arguments to prove that it is Paul's. At present I shall adduce from the Gospel what Jesus Christ testifies concerning the prophets, together with a story which He refers to, but which is not found in the Old Testament, since in it also there is a scandal against unjust judges in Israel. The words of our Savior run thus: "Woe unto you, scribes and Pharisees, hypocrites because ye build the tombs of the prophets, and garnish the sepulchers of the righteous, and say, If we had been in the days of our fathers, we would not have been partaken with them in the blood of the prophets. Wherefore be ye witnesses unto yourselves, that ye are the children of them which killed the prophets. Fill ye up then the measure of
your fathers. Ye serpents, ye generation of vipers, how can ye escape the damnation of Gehenna? Wherefore, behold, I send unto you prophets, and wise men, and scribes; and some
of them ye shall kill and crucify; and some of them shall ye scourge in your synagogues, and persecute them from city to city: that upon you may come all the righteous blood shed upon the earth, from the blood of righteous Abel unto the blood of Zacharias, son of Barachias, whom ye slew between the temple and the altar. Verily I say unto you, All these things shall come upon this generation." And what follows is of the same tenor: "O Jerusalem, Jerusalem, thou that kills the prophets, and stones them which are sent unto thee, how often would I have gathered thy children together, even as a hen gathers her

chickens under her wings, and ye would not! Behold, your house is left unto you desolate."

Let us see now if in these cases we are not forced to the conclusion, that while the Savior gives a true account of them, none of the Scriptures which could prove what He tells are to be found. For they who build the tombs of the prophets and garnish the sepulchers of the righteous, condemning the crimes their fathers committed against the righteous and the prophets, say, "If we had been in the days of our fathers, we would not have been partakers with them in the blood of the prophets." In the blood of what prophets, can anyone tell me? For where do we find anything like this written of Esaias, or Jeremias, or any of the twelve, or Daniel? Then about Zacharias the son of Barachias, who was slain between the temple and the altar, we learn from Jesus only, not knowing it otherwise from any Scripture. Wherefore I think no other supposition is possible, than that they who had the reputation of wisdom, and the rulers and elders, took away from the people every passage which might bring them into discredit among the people. We need not wonder, then, if this history of the evil device of the licentious elders against Susanna is true, but was concealed and removed from the Scriptures by men themselves not very far removed from the counsel of these elders.

In the Acts of the Apostles also, Stephen, in his other testimony, says, "Which of the prophets have not your fathers persecuted? And they have slain them which showed before of the coming of the Just One; of whom ye have been now the betrayers and murderers." That Stephen speaks the truth, everyone will admit who receives the Acts of the Apostles; but it is impossible to show from the extant books of the Old Testament how with any justice he throws the blame of having persecuted and slain the prophets on the fathers of those who believed not in Christ. And Paul, in the first Epistle to the Thessalonians, testifies this concerning the Jews: "For ye, brethren, became followers of the Churches of God which in Judea are in Christ Jesus: for ye also have suffered like things

A Letter from Origen to Africanus

of your own countrymen, even as they have of the Jews; who both killed the Lord Jesus and their own prophets, and have persecuted us; and they please not God, and are contrary to all men." What I have
said is, I think, sufficient to prove that it would be nothing wonderful if this history were true, and the licentious and cruel attack was actually made on Susanna by those who were
at that time elders, and written down by the wisdom of the Spirit, but removed by these rulers of Sodom, as the Spirit would call them.

10. Your next objection is, that in this writing Daniel is said to have been seized by the Spirit, and to have cried out that the sentence was unjust; while in that writing of his which
is universally received he is represented as prophesying in quite another manner, by visions and dreams, and an angel appearing to him, but never by prophetic inspiration. You seem to me to pay too little heed to the words, "At sundry times, and in divers manners, God spoke in time past unto the fathers by the prophets." This is true not only in the general, but also of individuals. For if you notice, you will find that the same saints have been favored with divine dreams and angelic appearances and (direct) inspirations. For the present it will suffice to instance what is testified concerning Jacob. Of dreams from God he speaks thus: "And it came to pass, at the time that the cattle conceived, that I saw them before my eyes in a dream, and, behold, the rams and he-goats which leaped upon the sheep and the goats, white-spotted, and speckled, and grisled. And the angel of God spoke unto me in a dream, saying, Jacob. And I said, What is it? And he said, Lift up thine eyes and see, the goats and rams leaping on the goats and sheep, white-spotted, and speckled, and grisled: for I have seen all that Laban doeth unto thee. I am God, who appeared unto thee in the place of God, where thou anointedst to Me there a pillar, and vowedst a vow there to Me: now arise, get thee out from this land, and return unto the land of thy kindred." And as to an appearance (which is better than a dream), he speaks as follows

about himself: "And Jacob was left alone; and there wrestled a man with him until the breaking of the day. And he saw that he prevailed not against him, and he touched the breadth of his thigh; and the breadth of Jacob's thigh grew stiff while he was wrestling with him. And he said to him, Let me go, for the day breaketh. And he said, I will not let thee go, except thou bless me. And he said unto him, What is thy name? And he said, Jacob. And he said to him, Thy name shall be called no more Jacob, but Israel shall be thy name: for thou hast prevailed with God, and art powerful with men. And Jacob asked him, and said, Tell me thy name. And he said, Wherefore is it that thou dost ask after my name? And he blessed him there. And Jacob called the name of the place Vision of God: for I have seen God face to face, and my life is preserved. And the sun rose, when the vision of God passed by." And that he also prophesied by inspiration, is evident from this passage: "And Jacob called unto his sons, and said, Gather yourselves together, that I may tell you what shall befall you
in the last days. Gather yourselves together, and hear, ye sons of Jacob; and hearken unto Israel your father. Reuben, my firstborn, my might, and the beginning of my children, hard to be born, hard and stubborn. Thou wert wanton, boil not over like water; because thou wentest up to thy father's bed; then defiledst thou the couch to which thou wentest up." And so with the rest: it was by inspiration that the prophetic blessings were pronounced. We need not wonder, then, that Daniel sometimes prophesied by inspiration, as when he rebuked the elders sometimes, as you say, by dreams and visions, and at other times by an angel appearing unto him.

    11. Your other objections are stated, as it appears to me, somewhat irreverently, and without the becoming spirit of piety. I cannot do better than quote your very words: "Then,
after crying out in this extraordinary fashion, he detects them in a way no less incredible, which not even Philistion the playwriter would have resorted to. For, not satisfied with rebuking them through the Spirit, he placed them apart, and asked them

severally where they saw her committing adultery; and when the one said, 'Under a holm-tree' (*prinos*) he answered that the angel would saw him asunder (*prisein*); and in a similar fashion threatened the other, who said, 'Under a mastich-tree' (*schinos*), with being rent asunder."

You might as reasonably compare to Philistion the play-writer, a story somewhat like this one, which is found in the third book of Kings, which you yourself will admit to be well written. Here is what we read in Kings:—

"Then there appeared two women that were harlots before the king, and stood before him. And the one woman said, To me, my lord, I and this woman dwell in one house; and we were delivered in the house. And it came to pass, the third day after that I was delivered, that this woman was delivered also: and we were together; there is no one in our house except us two. And this woman's child died in the night; because she overlaid it. And she arose at midnight, and took my son from my arms. And thine handmaid slept. And she laid it in her bosom, and laid her dead child in my bosom. And I arose in the morning to give my child suck, and he was dead; but when I had considered it in the morning, behold, it was not my son which I did bear. And the other woman said, Nay; the dead is thy son, but the living is my son. And the other said, No; the living is my son, but the dead is thy son. Thus they spoke before the king. Then said the king, Thou sayest, This is my son that liveth, and thy son is the dead: and thou sayest, Nay; but thy son is the dead, and my son is the living. And the king said, Bring me a sword. And they brought a sword before the king. And the king said, Divide the living child in two, and give half to the one, and half to the other. Then spoke the woman whose the living child was unto the king (for her bowels yearned after her son), and she said, To me, my lord, give her the living child, and in no wise slay it. But the other said, Let it be neither mine nor thine, but divide it. Then the king answered and said, Give the child to her which said, Give her the living child, and in no wise slay it: for she is the mother of it. And all Israel heard of the judgment which the king had judged; and they feared the face of the king: for they saw that the wisdom of God was in him to do judgment."

For if we were at liberty to speak in this scoffing way of the Scriptures in use in the Churches, we should rather compare this story of the two harlots to the play of Philistion than that of the chaste Susanna. And just as the people would not have been persuaded if Solomon had merely said, "Give this one the living child, for she is the mother of it;" so Daniel's attack on the elders would not have been sufficient had there not been added the condemnation from their own mouth, when both said that they had seen her lying with the young man under a tree, but did not agree as to what kind of tree it was. And since you have asserted, as if you knew for certain, that Daniel in this matter judged by inspiration (which may or may not have been the case), I would have you notice that there seem to me to be some analogies in the story of Daniel to the judgment of Solomon, concerning whom the Scripture testifies that the people saw that the wisdom of God was in him to do judgment. This might be said also of Daniel, for it was because wisdom was in him to do judgment that the elders were judged in the manner described.

12. I had nearly forgotten an additional remark I have to make about the *prino-prisein* and *schino-schisein* difficulty; that is, that in our Scriptures there are many etymological fancies, so to call them, which in the Hebrew are perfectly suitable, but not in the Greek. It need not surprise us, then, if the translators of the History of Susanna contrived it so that they found out some Greek words, derived from the same root, which either corresponded exactly to the Hebrew form (though this I hardly think possible), or presented some analogy to it. Here is an instance of this in our Scripture. When the woman was made by God from the rib of the man, Adam says, "She shall be called woman, because she was taken out of her husband." Now the Jews say that the woman was called

"*Essa*," and that "taken" is a translation of this word as is evident from "*chos isouoth essa*," which means, "I have taken the cup of salvation;" and that "*is*" means "man," as we see from "*Hesre aïs*," which is, "Blessed is the man." According to the Jews, then, "*is*" is "man," and "*essa*," "woman," because she was taken out of her husband (*is*). It need not then surprise us if some interpreters of the Hebrew "Susanna," which had been concealed among them at a very remote date, and had been preserved only by the more learned and honest, should have either given the Hebrew word for word, or hit upon some analogy to the Hebrew forms, that the Greeks might be able to follow them. For in many other passages we can find traces of this kind of contrivance on the part of the translators, which I noticed when I was collating the various editions.

13. You raise another objection, which I give in your own words: "Moreover, how is it that they, who were captives among the Chaldeans, lost and won at play, thrown out unburied on the streets, as was prophesied of the former captivity, their sons torn from them to be eunuchs, and their daughters to be concubines, as had been prophesied; how is it that such could pass sentence of death, and that on the wife of their king Joakim, whom the king of the Babylonians had made partner of his throne? Then, if it was not this Joakim, but some other from the common people, whence had a captive such a mansion and spacious garden?"

Where you get your "lost and won at play, and thrown out unburied on the streets," I know not, unless it is from Tobias; and Tobias (as also Judith), we ought to notice, the Jews do not use. They are not even found in the Hebrew Apocrypha, as I learned from the Jews themselves. However, since the Churches use Tobias, you must know that even in the captivity some of the captives were rich and well to do. Tobias himself says, "Because I remembered God with all my heart; and the Most High gave me grace and beauty in the eyes of Nemessarus, and I was his purveyor; and I went into Media, and left in trust with Gabael, the brother of Gabrias, at Ragi, a city of Media, ten talents of silver." And he adds, as if he were a rich man, "In the days of Nemessarus I gave many alms to my brethren. I gave my bread to the hungry, and my clothes to the naked: and if I saw any of my nation dead, and cast outside the walls of Nineve, I buried him; and if king Senachereim had slain any when he came fleeing from Judea, I buried them privily (for in his wrath he killed many)." Think whether this great catalogue of Tobias's good deeds does not betoken great wealth and much property, especially when he adds, "Understanding that I was sought for to be put to death, I withdrew myself for fear, and all my goods were forcibly taken away."

And another captive, Dachiacharus, the son of Ananiel, the brother of Tobias, was set over all the exchequer of the kingdom of king Acherdon; and we read, "Now Achiacharus was cup-bearer and keeper of the signet, and steward and overseer of the accounts."

Mardochaios, too, frequented the court of the king, and had such boldness before him, that he was inscribed among the benefactors of Artaxerxes.

Again we read in Esdras, that Neemias, a cup-bearer and eunuch of the king, of Hebrew race, made a request about the rebuilding of the temple, and obtained it; so that it was granted to him, with many more, to return and build the temple again. Why then should we wonder that one Joakim had garden, and house, and property, whether these were very expensive or only moderate, for this is not clearly told us in the writing?

14. But you say, "How could they who were in captivity pass sentence of death?" asserting, I know not on what grounds, that Susanna was the wife of a king, because of the name Joakim. The answer is, that it is no uncommon thing, when great nations become subject, that the king should allow the captives to use their own laws and courts of justice. Now, for instance, that the Romans rule, and the Jews pay the half-shekel to them, how great power by the concession of Cæsar

the ethnarch has; so that we, who have had experience of it, know that he differs in little from a true king! Private trials are held according to the law, and some are condemned to death. And though there is not full license for this, still it is not done without the knowledge of the ruler, as we learned and were convinced of when we spent much time in the country of that people. And yet the Romans only take account of two tribes, while at that time besides Judah there were the ten tribes of Israel. Probably the Assyrians contented themselves with holding them in subjection, and conceded to them their own judicial processes.

15. I find in your letter yet another objection in these words: "And add, that among all the many prophets who had been before, there is no one who has quoted from another word for word. For they had no need to go a-begging for words, since their own were true. But this one, in rebuking one of these men, quotes the words of the Lord, 'The innocent and righteous shalt thou not slay.'" I cannot understand how, with all your exercise in investigating and meditating on the Scriptures, you have not noticed that the prophets continually quote each other almost word for word. For who of all believers does not know the words in Esaias? "And in the last days the mountain of the Lord shall be manifest, and the house of the Lord on the top of the mountains, and it shall be exalted above the hills; and all nations shall come unto it. And many people shall go and say, Come ye, and let us go up to the mountain of the Lord, unto the house of the God of Jacob; and He will teach us His way, and we will walk in it: for out of Zion shall go forth a law, and a word of the Lord from Jerusalem. And He shall judge among the nations, and shall rebuke many people; and they shall beat their swords into ploughshares, and their spears into pruning-hooks: nation shall not lift up sword against nation; neither shall they learn war anymore."

But in Micah we find a parallel passage, which is almost word for word: "And in the last days the mountain of the Lord shall be manifest, established on the top of the mountains, and it shall be exalted above the hills; and people shall hasten unto it. And many nations shall come, and say, Come, let us go up to the mountain of the Lord, to the house of the God of Jacob; and they will teach us His way, and we will walk in His paths: for a law shall go forth from Zion, and a word of the Lord from Jerusalem. And He shall judge among many people, and rebuke strong nations; and they shall beat their swords into ploughshares, and their spears into pruning-hooks: nation shall not lift up a sword against nation, neither shall they learn war anymore."

Again, in First Chronicles, the psalm which is put in the hands of Asaph and his brethren to praise the Lord, beginning, "Give thanks unto the Lord, call upon His name," is in the beginning almost identical with Psalm cv., down to "and do my prophets no harm;" and after that it is the same as Psalm xcvi., from the beginning of that psalm, which is something like this, "Praise the Lord all the earth," down to "For He cometh to judge the earth." (It would have taken up too much time to quote more fully; so I have given these short references, which are sufficient for the matter before us.) And you will find the law about not bearing a burden on the Sabbath-day in Jeremias, as well as in Moses. And the rules about the Passover, and the rules for the priests, are not only in Moses, but also at the end of Ezekiel. I would have quoted these, and many more, had I not found that from the shortness of my stay in Nicomedia my time for writing you was already too much restricted.

Your last objection is, that the style is different. This I cannot see.

This, then, is my defense. I might, especially after all these accusations, speak in praise of this history of Susanna, dwelling on it word by word, and expounding the exquisite nature of the thoughts. Such an encomium, perhaps, some of the learned and able students of divine things may at some other time compose. This, however, is my answer to your strokes, as you call them. Would that I could instruct you! But I do not now arrogate that to myself. My lord and dear brother Ambrosius, who has written this at my dictation, and has, in looking over it, corrected as he pleased, salutes you. His faithful spouse, Marcella, and her children, also salute you. Also Anicetus. Do you salute our dear father Apollinarius, and all our friends.

www.ingramcontent.com/pod-product-compliance
Lightning Source LLC
Chambersburg PA
CBHW052043070526
44584CB00018B/2585